Evincepub
Publishing

Evincepub Publishing

Parijat Extension, Bilaspur, Chhattisgarh 495001
First Published By Evincepub Publishing 2021
Copyright © Dr Anu Girdhar 2021
All Rights Reserved.

ISBN: 978-93-5446-089-0

As the life
Unfolds

Dr Anu Girdhar

I dedicate this book to my loving parents,

My biggest support my husband Dr Puneet Girdhar,

My children Aarushi and Aaryan.

Foreword

'Expressive poetry' needs expertise in recording life experiences and common observations. Micro analysis of a surrounding is what a writer is composed of, in terms of individual talent. It wouldn't be surprising if I could say at this juncture, that a writer is mostly enlightened when he or she goes far beyond from what a simple mind can handle. The invocation of cosmic gift such as poetry needs a mind that circumspect farther from the common man's purview. Thus poetry has ever been a human solace in times of isolation or leisure. The readers grab those verses with the greed that one has, while wishing to devour their favorite culinary choices. The words that connect and relay wisdom, keeps the reader salivating to read more. Thus a life experience written in poetic verses, can earnestly penetrate all the chambers of a reader's mind.

When Dr Anu Girdhar approached me with a request for this foreword, I was under the impression that this would be another theme based poetry book to endorse. But I was mistaken; this book titled 'AS THE LIFE UNFOLDS' does speak the streamlined record of a full woman's life in verse form. Doing one round of reading the content and the poems in it, took me back to those years when I was searching for an identity which I wasn't sure ever existed. The first poem 'Once Upon a Time' does reflect many verses where the reader can connect to reality, that too with amusement playing the role of muse throughout the book. These simple verses speak an epic when read with perception

*"Being soft and gentle didn't mean she was not strong,
She was the sunshine mixed with storm"*

Many times it would be frivolous to judge a person by his
or her outward appearance or personality. Moods of
others can help an onlooker to get closer to a character
analysis, however it's still a bud stage that needs lot of
interactions for it to bloom as character judgement.
Character of a second person can only be read when one
is patient, shows respect, love and mutual concern to that
person. This entire book reveals the story of a woman who
has much more to speak apart from judged humility and
simplicity. It reflects a woman's search for life's core
values to cherish. The book has lots to speak about the
protagonist, which weaves a connected bond in 91 poems
completing 5 chapters or rather five powerful hurdles in
life such as 'evolution, education, challenge, family and
quest for self actualization'.

Another thing which definitely needs to be highlighted
with binocular eyes about this book is the wisdom rich
verses that make up its content.

*"Two birds never sing the same song,
Your right can be my wrong."*

These verses speak broader essays on human differences,
and more on their judgmental paradox. That's why
humans are mostly known as Homo sapiens. If we all
collectively sing the same song, the whole world would
have decided to forego the melody of its life process. So
objections, questions and queries are a part of human
nature. It can be to the surrounding or to oneself. It helps
in railing the mind to wiser revelations and consolations.
Being a daughter, mother, wife and a professional is the
unique strength found in the cosmic wonder called

woman. This book does unveil broader reasoning to such simple fact, which is mostly ignored by the masculine egos. Well, this book did keep me engrossed till the last page, with thrill and curiosity, being my mood appetizer. I was amazed by Author Anu Girdhar's understanding of life's relevance, and each poem stands a testimonial to brain and emotional development.

'I yearn to break free,
I crave to fly high,
I want to enjoy the freedom to be me."

Well, the above verse clears a long pending cobweb which is there in most of us humans, despite the fact that we are many at times reasonable to oneself and known to self as the wonder sapiens (wise). Now flip the pages ahead and read on. This book by Dr Anu Girdhar titled 'AS THE LIFE UNFOLDS' does unfold rich poetry. It will unfold a world which existed around you, but will take this book to realize it better. Poetry couldn't have been better...

Regards
Shiju H. Pallithazheth
* Author of Best Seller 'Katashi Tales and 'The Ghost Wisdom'
* Founder - Motivational Strips
* Co - World Nations Writers Union
* Global Advisor - Lasosyasyon Lar Sans Frontyer
* Managing Editor - The Genius

• • •
x

Contents Table

Chapter: 5 Middle Age

Once Upon A Time

Once Upon A Time

Once Upon A Time
There was a girl, shy and introvert,
A girl who wanted you to start the conversation first.
The girl who was quiet with people she didn't know,
But crazy in front of friends who were close,
Being soft and gentle didn't mean she was not strong,
She was the sunshine mixed with storm.
She was actually the queen of her own orb.
She had a smile, only one of a kind,
Honesty was not just her nature, it was a way of life,
Every shy girl can have a wild side,
Quiet people can have the loudest minds.

Anu Girdhar

The Journey Begins

The journey of life started with little steps,
College: A place where two strangers met,
And turned out to be family at the end,
In between freshers and farewell, life happened.

College life was like no other time in life,
College inspired her, gave her confidence.

In college they made the memories of life time,
College gave them their occupation,
prepared them to face life.

College Time

Those five years of college,
Daily morning alarm, beautiful dresses,
Meeting, chatting, sitting next to our friends.

No mobiles, still we were happy,
Our friendship was our therapy.

Millions of memories, thousands of jokes,
hundreds of secrets,
A place from where I got my best friend.

Exams, viva, so many assignments,
Eventually everything came to an end.

The friends we made in college are friends for life,
Even if we don't talk for years at a time.

Anu Girdhar

First Love Letter

In college, I got to write my first love letter.

That hand written letter,
I took whole day to write,
The letter filled with emotions,
the glory of expression and some sunshine.

In that letter I wanted him to know,
I become a little weak when it comes to speak,
I can't express what I feel,
So I write on paper,
My emotions, my hopes and my dreams.

Love

The words I never said but you heard,
That therapeutic power of your silent touch,
That conversation between our minds,
That unknown feeling, so divine,
Our thoughts translated into breeze,
Travelled afar,
There was telepathy between our hearts.

Language of Love

A truth that doesn't speak,
A lie that doesn't deceive,
A simple smile, a tender touch,
A language not spoken, but you can feel,
The language of love that you and me can perceive.

Love is the language I write into,
Expression of words it doesn't need,
Falling in love is like learning a new language,
The language in which you and me dream.

Love has no barrier, no limit,
Hearts know how to communicate with feels,
Love doesn't care what religion you believe,
Love has its own vibration,
Let it be the only vibration that we breathe in.

Moonless Night

In that dark moonless night as he held her tight,
He found moon in her eyes.

His love was so deep,
loved her darker side,
Her secrets, her emotions, her vibes,
She too loved his demons, drove him wild.

She stared at him in that moonless night,
As she forgot her pain, was little terrified,
Terrified of losing herself again.

In that dark, they saw some stars,
She didn't need him to light her world,
She wanted him to sit with her in the dark.

His love was not blind,
He saw her in the dark,
And chose to be her light.

Anu Girdhar

Wedding Bells

Today surrounded by the ones we love,
We vow to honour, inspire and respect each other
for the rest of our days,
Long ago you were just a dream,
A dream for which I used to pray,
Today I stand before you,
Lost in my thoughts,
Short of right words to say.
My best friend,
My brightest love,
My dear husband.

Knot

With trust and love,
I shall keep the knot tight,
I LOVE U
And I will always love you,
even when the times are not right.

Anu Girdhar

Lost And Drowned

Yours is the light, underneath my spirit blooms,
Dance in its dazzle, obliviates gloom.
Hand in hand, by the moonlight,
Kiss me with passion, hold me tight.
The twinkle of my love, reflection of my heart
Lost and drowned,
O'my moon, doesn't want to be found.

Marriage

Best friends for life,
Husband and wife.
Marriage, a long journey,
On love and commitment, it thrives.

Marriage doesn't guarantee togetherness,
It needs love, respect and trust to survive.

Marriage doesn't mean,
You and me will always agree,
Or see eye to eye,
If we care, we shall probably fight.

Marriage means never giving up on the relationship,
Never making each other cry.

Anu Girdhar

Romance in Rain

He was the rain, she being the earth,
That earthy scent, when they met.
The psithurism all around,
Seducing her with rhythmic sound.

That unpredictable, unseasonal fall,
Falling on her parched soul,
Kissing her, making her alive,
Getting drained in that rain,
Rain of that fresh start, taking away all her pain.

Wrapped around each other,
Drenched in those moments of glee,
He made love to her,
The way rain made love to trees.

Love Is In The Air

Love is a promise,
love is a prayer;
Love is surrender,
love is souvenir.

Love makes me free from all the pain,
Falling on my parched heart, drenching it in rain.

Your words are my food, your breath is my wine,
Your love is a feeling so divine.

The pleasing song of love that I sing every day,
With every rhythmic note, miseries are swept away.

The castle of my dreams that I build with your love,
nurtured with the blessings,
bestowed from above.

Our love is so simple,
It's my coffee and your tea,
Some moments filled with warmth,
Some filled with glee.

Anu Girdhar

Motherhood

A mother is born,
before the child is born.

Carrying a baby in the womb and under the heart,
A journey of lifetime's love is about to start.

At a first glance, she is surprised at her creation,
Full of love and joy,
she feels as if she is a magician.

In her children, she finds love that is
pure and unconditional,
She stands with them like a rock
which is additional.

Motherhood, where all the blessings and love
begin and end,
Not only your mom, with time she becomes your
best friend.

Love droops, youth evaporates,
It's only mother's love that always radiates.

Life doesn't come with a manual, it comes with a
mother,
Shower her with love as you will not find another.

My Child

My Child! No one could ever love you the way I do,
The journey of this love began,
before the birth of you.

In my womb and your image on screen,
I saw you, my heart skipped a beat.

Took all the pains and cut my cord,
O'my God!
This tiny bundle
A piece of magic, what I felt,
I never forgot.

You grew up fast and went to school,
The first time I parted with you,
Those three hours, I know what I went through.

Feeding you and teaching you was my only passion,
Always jubilant and blissful to see your
progression.

You blossomed into a pretty girl/handsome hunk,
Time took you in the teenage world.
That sparkling world blurred your vision,
In wonder land and exploration,
Your mom is always there to clear the confusion.

You are the greatest thing that ever happened in my
life,
I bless you, love you and will always do till I am
alive.

You are the first thing,
I think of every morning,
And the first thing I pray for each night,
I seek your love, respect and warmth,
In you I found the love of my life.

———∿∿∿———

18

As The Time Revolved

Anu Girdhar

The Girl In Her Evolved

As the time revolved,
The girl in her evolved.

Her evolution from a shy, introvert girl,
To a woman full of self-love,
Now with full energy she swirls.

No doubt many obstacles she faced,
But she moved ahead with strength and grace.

She was a daughter, a wife and a mother,
But craved for her identity, her own face.

She learnt more from failures than from success,
In her journey she encountered many defeats,
faced lot of stress.

She desired to be a rainbow in thick clouds,
Her confidence was her best friend.

Her power of imagination was infinite,
She travelled through her madness,
at last found herself.
In search of sunshine, she herself became the one.

Her mission in life was not only to survive,
It was to thrive with success

Virgo Woman

A Virgo woman, the real deal,
To protect herself from hurt,
around her a wall she builds,
Her mind is always on overdrive,
though she may look calm and at ease,
She is a lover loyal to the core,
an independent woman indeed.

A Virgo woman,
having the backbone of steel,
For her love means the true love,
no other definition of love she feels,
She is diligent and hardworking
who faces new challenges with zeal,
She is usually blunt with weapons in her mouth,
a transparent soul,
whose charisma no one can steal.

Anu Girdhar

Vagabond Spirit

Hidden deep down,
Her vagabond spirit,
Singing the songs of unknown lyrics.
Flying high in sky, with her Cape,
She neither surrenders nor escapes.

Lust To Wander

Lust to wander and explore the world,
To make memories, to be adventurous,
to know the worth,
Yearn to fly, to travel, to roam,
Looking deep in nature,
Leaving footprints on the unknown road.

Anu Girdhar

Self Love

Its not selfish when you love yourself my dear,
As the love you crave for is rare.

Be the love, the one you always desired,
Discover the strength you always acquired.

You are Amazing! You are Beautiful!
You are Positive!
Give yourself grace and respect
that's your prerogative!!

Your imperfections make you Special and Unique,
Derive pleasure from the silence that speaks.

Ever talked to yourself ? it never goes in vain,
Soul is enlightened, gaining strength from pain.

Learn to sail your ship, don't be afraid of storm,
Breathe in, breathe out and move on.

Dream without fear, love without limit,
Sparkle in self-love, no one can dim it.

Challenges Of Life

How shall we grow,
If we didn't face the challenges,
We didn't struggle in life.
Her battles made her realise,
She has to bear the burdens of her own soul,
When she cries, she has to cry alone.
Looking in mirror, with tears in eyes,
Waiting for the pain to subside,
Perfecting the balance between struggle and life,
She learnt how to survive.

Growing Together

Deep in the darkness,
Merged together,
They chose to be each other's light,
Darkness that frightened,
Darkness so silent,
The darkness was lit by her love,
Made it bright.
As love is meeting of two souls,
Fully accepting the light and dark both.

Being Positive

You turn out to be what you believe,
It's not about good or bad,
It's about how you perceive.

When you feed your mind with faith and trust,
Train your heart to forget the worst,
Teach your eyes to see the best,
Whatever is the situation, you learn to accept,
Peace begins, you feel blessed.

You got to believe,
Your morning is good,
Your life is a bliss.

When the smallest and most mundane
things excite you,
You really know how to live,
Happiness is a choice,
Train your mind to see good in
whatever you receive.

Anu Girdhar

Celebrate The Differences

Two birds never sing the same song,
Your right can be my wrong.
When we share our similarities,
But celebrate our differences,
It really makes our relation strong.

We can never make this difference as a matter of
conflict,
We accept our perspectives, our realities with
peace,
Not everyone thinks the way we think,
Believes the way we believe.

Being together, seeing together,
My soul accepts you as whole,
We differ in perceptions,
Accepting the difference, give different reactions,
You and me if desire to stay together,
Difference in opinion doesn't matter.

A great marriage doesn't bring two perfect people
together,
It's when an imperfect couple learns to enjoy their
differences.

Ups And Downs

Anu Girdhar

Storm

Storm that's inside,
Storm that needs respite,
Some unanswered questions,
Those sharp words of loved ones,
Piercing through the soul,
That indifferent attitude,
She is hanging on.
Some solace she requires,
Some warmth she desires,
Some courage and strength she hires,
To ignore, to perceive silence,
To detach.

Respect, words that make her inside calm,
Those words she seeks,
Is it only her call,
To make all happy and united,
What about her own storm,
She is fighting with day and night.

When no one listens, she writes,
On the heart of that blank paper,
Her feelings, her desires,
This paper is her new friend,
that lends her a shoulder, when she cries.

The Wall

The walls she has built-up around herself,
The walls that are mysterious and tall,
The walls so high and cold,
The walls that existed as she let them grow,
The walls she built up over a life time,
stone by stone,
Either to climb or to remain attached to these walls,
Or is she waiting for someone to knock.
She looks forward for the kind of love,
that could penetrate these walls.
She wants these walls to come down,
Desires love to take over,
Longs to lose her control.

Anu Girdhar

Communication In Relationship

Relationship needs communication and trust,
Speak up, don't let it rust.

Distance doesn't separate you and me,
Silence does.
Sometimes it hurts more than words.

Physically together but emotionally apart,
Let's mend our ways before withering starts.

It's not love that needs to be chased,
Set it free.
If it comes back with heart and soul,
it should be braced.

Silence will not let love survive.
Communicate, it's oxygen to life.

Love is not between you and me,
It's between our hearts.
Let it flow with glee

Words

Ever considered the power of words?
Words can heal the soul,
Words can create the hurt.
Words have the ability to transform your life,
They can also transform someone's world.

Words can do wonders,
They can also make the heart surrender.

Be impeccable, Be sure what you say,
Be careful what you plant,
be careful what you convey.
Speech has power, words don't fade,
After a dark night,
some soulful words can brighten someone's day.

Have you ever talked to yourself?
Have you ever expressed yourself in words?
Trust me, it never goes in vain,
It leaves the deep impact, it relieves the pain.

Anu Girdhar

Fire Within

Nothing new to watch, no matter how much you
may revisit the past,
To light a fire within, you just need a spark.

The spark that could ignite the fire of your heart,
The fire that shines so bright,
You could see your way out of dark.

The fire of desires, that was always there,
Now let it glow,
These burning desires will help the life
to take its flow.

Wipe your tears,
Shine through your fears,
You were always full of strength and fierce.

You were capable of more than you knew,
Now the dreams are lit, build from it.

No need to see the milestone,
Now you can't postpone,
You don't require approval,
This is the journey of your desires and your dreams.
Move ahead, be strong,
You come and leave the world alone.

• • •

Woman

Half woman, half warrior,
combination of delicate and strong,
beautiful and fierce, love and care,
sacrifice and share,
desiring the respect, is it that so rare.

To her respect comes before love and attention,
Beware of a silent smiling woman
as she knows your intention

She never forgets the people who were always
there for her
Loving, caring and sharing is so natural and she will
never let it blur

Why you judge her by the looks and attire
Saree, suit or skirt she can wear as per her desire

When she stands up for herself, she stands up for
all the women
The one beautiful woman you would definitely
admire

Respect her before you love her
That's what she always aspires

Anu Girdhar

Before I Die

Find me before I cry,
Love me before I die

Love made me happy, love gave me hope,
Loved you with my mind, with my heart and
my soul.

Love was not perfect, it was real,
Love was forever, why it disappeared.
Got busy with things to do, whenever stopped
thought of you,
With lost chemistry, love was lost and it flew.

Love is a journey, starting at forever,
ending at never,
Needs the one, scared of losing it ever.

Before I die, tell those words I want to hear,
When I die, don't come to my grave and
shed your tears.

First love never dies, forced love can bury it alive.

Give Time To Your Relations

Give time to your relations
Expressions to your words,
Mumtaz didn't see Taj Mahal,
Taj Mahal was seen by the world,
Love me now,
I want to bask in its rays,
Visit The Taj Mahal in me today.

Handwritten Love Letters

Handwritten love letters of my first love,
Engraved innocent words of that pristine love,
The love of our tender age,
The age where we both were so naive.
The first touch, when your love touched my skin,
The first kiss, when your lips tasted my lips
First I LOVE YOU made my heart swing on the
stars,
First glance that peeped inside my soul,
Our first hearty laugh was blissful and pure,
My dear lover, when you held me so close,
Those moments of our first love, still etched on my
heart
Now I am wandering and looking for them alone,
Where have they gone.

Introspection

Introspection

Perfectly imperfect, she was a little insane,
Unfilled expectations gave her pain.

Her brightened face,
lit with spirit of a kid,
Love didn't hurt her, expectations did.

She feared rejection,
craved affection,
Her grief was her inspiration.

Putting her pieces together, she had self-reflection,
Used her intuition for introspection.

She loved the sound of feet, moving away from
pathless roads,
Questioning herself, had a deeper look at her
instincts.

Evaluation of path was the first step forward,
She evolved herself,
open to critics.

She suddenly knew,
It's time to start afresh,
She learnt her lessons and grew from it.
Now writing is her catharsis, a journey within.

She

She was lonely but never alone,
She was weak but felt strong,
She was sad but she laughed.
Bold enough to raise her voice,
Brave enough to rejoice.

She went that extra mile, there was no crowd.
She learnt her lessons and felt proud.

Happiness was her make-up,
Grace was her style.
Confidence changed her game,
Loved the person she became.

Tears rolled down her heart.
She didn't apologize,
For being sensitive,
Strong enough to erase the negative.

Master Your Own Life

You can't let anyone else hold the pen,
When it's the story of your life,
It's your prerogative to write it from the beginning
till the end.
Get up, take the charge of your happiness,
Choose what to let go and what to accept.
Have the courage to design your destiny yourself.

Tinker Around

Have faith and tinker around,
Embrace your life with little sound,
Take up the challenge, give it a wink,
Get up, dress up never rethink,
Follow the dreams with pixie dust,
Conquer the world with faith and trust,
Don't lose your sparkle, let it reflect,
Magic happens when you least expect.

Thoughts

Trapped Inside My Own Thoughts
Me, my freedom, my happiness, my whole lot,
Trapped inside my own soul,
I check between right and wrong.

Trying to escape from the dark clutches,
Of my mind, I am caged in,
I yearn to break free,
I crave to fly high,
I want to enjoy the freedom to be me.

Silence That Speaks

That deep silence, those warm tears,
Tears of approval, silence of acceptance,
Silence that screams,
Silence that roars,
That silence she wore.

The ripples of silence making sound,
Silence, so freaking loud,
The echo of silence that resonates
louder than words,
When ricochets, bliss and peace is conferred.

Loving her silently, loving her with soul,
Wiping her tears, kissing her flaws,
making her whole.

Truth is silent, creation is silent,
Silently it grows.

Anu Girdhar

Living On The Edge

Learn to live on the edge, learn to live through your
fears.
It might take lot of nerve, lot of energy O' my dear.
You can't let the expectations and aspirations of
others affect you,
Be a warrior, whenever you want you can put your
life back in the gear.

Be brave, when you are scared,
Be strong, when you are weak,
Trust yourself,
Whatever you decide you can achieve.
Do what matters most to you,
The joy of life comes from your encounters,
experiences and feels.
If living on the edge makes you alive,
makes you happy,
Just explore, discover and dream.
Prioritize yourself as your life is supreme,
The biggest adventure is to live
the life of your dreams.

Imperfectly Perfect

She is beautiful with her flaws, with her mistakes,
But inspired those who had no hope, no faith.

She fights when nothing goes right,
She spills the things and clumsy slight.

Her hair too never stay in place,
But she hugs her fallibilities with grace.

There is a crack in everything,
That's how the light gets in.
Her light is breath-taking,
Her aura is captivating.

She is magic, she is an exception who doesn't fear
rejection,
As beauty lies in heart and perception.

Her imperfections beautify her soul,
She embraces her flaws like thorns in a rose.

Anu Girdhar

Poetess In Her

A poetess in her shuts her eyes in order to visualise,
Countless stories, she fantasize.

How sun loved the moon, to an extent,
To let her breathe, he died every night.

Life, the wonderful fantasy in itself,
And fantasy, the origin of marvel,
scripting her emptiness,
Drunk with such poetry, she is immersed in herself.

Her poems are blooded with emotions,
some delicate and tough skin of words she inks,
Words that unzip the heartstrings,
She wants you to read those words and hear her
voice within.

Her words give her solace, they are herself rewards,
Soaked in them, her spirit learnt to sing.

Poetry

Poetry an ancient art, a language of heart,
A rhythmical creation of beauty in expression,
Originates from the flow of thoughts,
Some unsaid words, highest emotions and
controlled desires.
When she controls her desires,
She writes on the blank paper,
Her dreams, her hopes and her satires.

Anu Girdhar

I, Me, Myself

I am me and it's very pleasant,
Rejoicing the past, I live in present.

Liable for my strokes, whatever may come,
dancing to the beats of my own drum.

Confidence is my ability,
My happiness, my responsibility.

As you need air to breathe,
I need some time alone,
Time to be with me, to write, to feel strong.

Writing gives words to my silence,
Answers to my questions,
Shape to my expression,
Reality to my fantasy.

I won't insult me, by envying you,
You are splendid, I compliment you.

There are lots of people, I respect, I admire,
I am me, myself lighting my fire.

My improvement begins with I,
As I sing, dance and sway,
A better me is on the way.

Life Is A Bliss

You got to believe, your morning is good,
Your life is bliss.
It's not that how the life happens,
it's how you perceive.
When the smallest and most mundane things excite
you,
You really know how to live,
Happiness is a choice,
Train your mind to see good in whatever you
receive.

Boundless, Infinite

When I open the windows of my soul and my mind,
To let some fresh air come inside,
With my wings, that were already there
I let my dreams take a flight.
I just want to sit and see through the window,
To listen to my soul,
Fall asleep when moon is high in the sky.
A simple life,
I want to be boundless, infinite.

Surrender

When I released my resistance,
Love I perceived.

When I embraced the memories of my past,
And surrendered to my grief,
I moved from upheaval to inner peace.

When my ego surrendered to sovereignty,
Despair and fear dissolved,
My spirit surmised divinity.

I didn't surrender to love,
I became love in surrender.

That beautiful surrender of my soul to your
paradisiacal soul,
A salacious surrender, where I was lost,
Surrender that quenched my thirst,
Thirst for love, thirst for your therapeutic touch.

Anu Girdhar

Middle Age

Age

As I aged, many things changed,
Memories appeared in the wrinkles of my face,
My best friends, my will and my grace.

First I used to beg and chase,
Now out of this rat race,
I sit in corner and observe,
The nature, the beauty, the love,
I shall get what I deserve.

As I gather some more years,
Happiness is my makeup,
Silence I wear, some unsaid words I hear.
Now I am old enough to be less critical,
And young enough not to care.

Peace

When you train your mind to process life as it is,
When you let go of people who poison your spirit,
When you set peace of mind as the highest goal,
When you tame your desires, accept your role,
When you get detached from the strings and
possessed by nothing,
You are on the path of serenity,
Inner peace it brings.

Peace of mind that is beyond any victory or defeat,
It's not absence of conflict,
Its ability to deal with it.

When you free yourself from the resentful thoughts,
Choose to walk away from the doors that are closed,
Flow with time as it takes its course,
You achieve the peace of mind, health of soul.

Dreams

I have so many dreams that are worth
more than my sleep,
I dream to wander, to explore the world,
To make memories,
to be adventurous to know the worth,
I yearn to fly, to travel, to roam,
Looking deep in nature, leaving footprints on the
unknown road.

Hidden deep down, is my vagabond spirit,
Who sings the songs of unknown lyrics.
My dream is not to be popular,
to be perfect or to be rich,
It is to touch the lives of others without any hitch.

I surround myself with dreamers, the doers,
I surround myself with those who trust and really
believe in me.

I dream to be sun to lighten your life,
And to be moon to brighten the dark sky,
I dream for love, harmony and peace,
I dream this planet, a happy place,
I dream this world to be disease free.

Anu Girdhar

God

The light, the strength,
The master planner, whose plans we can't
understand.

He gives more than we imagine,
Hears more than we say,
He has his own time, his own way.

The lighthouse of God captivates us all,
As we sail through the sea of life,
Pass through storms.
In the cruel, insensitive world,
He is a glimpse of hope.

A good book, a companion or a mentor,
To light our paths in the dark,
He may come in any form.

My lord, my saviour,
He holds, whenever I fall,
When broken, he puts me back together,
He makes me walk, when I am not even
able to crawl.

My redemption comes from him,
My soul finds rest in God.

Middle Age

Middle age bubbling with confidence,
is a work of art
Beginning of anything you want,
When the relationship between body, mind and
the spirit starts.

A crossroad at which you are invited to release your
baggage and beliefs,
Stepping into your strength, paving a path for your
soul to heal.

A beautiful process whereby
you shed the layers of ego,
And decide to be at peace.

Physical attraction is no longer enough,
Genuine connection to undress the layers of soul
it needs.

When you desire to look like you,
Your Wrinkles indicate where the smiles have been,
No longer interested to look younger,
Healthy and radiant you aspire to be,
You become the person you always
should have been.

Anu Girdhar

You come to a point where you let go of what no
longer serves you,
A point where the freedom begins.

✺

Happiness

Sometimes a feeling, sometimes a decision,
And she decided to inspire before she expired,
She was strong willed to design a life that
she always aspired.

She was no longer available to meet their
expectations and disgrace,
She realised that only control she had,
was how she chose to face,
She made the decision to survive using
courage, humour and grace,
Ghosts, vampires and devils
didn't scare her,
She was affrighted of a cruel heart, devoid of love,
As the real monsters have always worn a
human face.

She surmised that the only person who could make
her happy was herself,
As happiness is not something readymade,
Happiness is self-created, it's a direction not a place,
She was the queen of her own life,
Her life was the choices she made.

Anu Girdhar

Beginning Of New Life

Today, a new day, a new year,
New hopes, new blessings,
For which I am thankful from my heart.
It's not just another day,
It's another chance.

With power to cope with clashes of past,
Enjoy the present, its not that hard.
Learn to let it go, it will change the game,
As things of past, belong to memory lane,
Present is a point, when time touches eternity,
You are just a decision away from infinity,
You can't be happy, if you see the past,
You are meant to live life of purpose,
believe in heart.

Look back with a smile,
If things didn't work out,
Make a fresh start.

Little is required to make your life happy,
It's all within you, in your positive approach and
in your thinking.

Winter Morning

When sunlight pierces through my dreams,
A warm hug, a bright smile, a cup of coffee,
that's what I need,
The morning glory on your face,
Your positive vibes warm my day,
A sated smile from naughty play,
You and cold winter mornings
are my best soul mates.

Anu Girdhar

Being Insane

I love being crazy, you may call me insane,
Crossing a turmoil, I found myself,
now I am hurricane.

Insanity did something great,
It rejuvenated the mind,
Made the mysteries disappear,
now life stands explained.

When normal gets boring,
And lacks imagination,
I go back to being me,
That's little insane.

My perception governs my happiness,
When it crawls inside my mind,
My fantasy goes wild.

I don't go crazy,
I just go normal,
From time to time.

Insanity is super sanity,
Taking things seriously is a serious waste of time.

Flowers

Her love like some fresh flowers,
Surged out of sombre hours,
Enchantment of those beautiful flowers,
Ecstasy, aroma of that beautiful shower.

Anu Girdhar

Friends

Who are you to me?

You are my pals and my buddies,
My companions and my best friends.

Meeting you was not an accident,
We met to laugh, cry, share, care, play, travel and
stick together.

Moments we spent and the lessons we learnt,
Are etched on the pages of my heart that can
never be burnt.

Our friendship is an emotional bond,
An experience that refreshes our souls.

We lift each other when we are tense,
We laugh and have fun even when it doesn't
make any sense.

My friends when you join my weirdness,
The moments are priceless and without any
pretence.

When things go wrong and I am confused,
what to do,
I just know that I can run to you.

You all hold me, love me,
No questions asked, no conditions applied and
no judgements passed.

Anu Girdhar

My Coffee Shop

My dream, my coffee shop,
A cosy place, a happy spot.
Where friends would come, talk and laugh,
Some crazy moments, captured in photographs.

As the time revolves, and the life dissolves,
Stop a while, come with me in coffee shop,
Coffee is a feeling, gives lot of hope.

Time is free, but can't be kept,
It can be cherished, if well spent.
Meet some people, make some friends.

Coffee, a book and some rays of sun,
Unexpected friendships are the best ones.

Here love and laughter is never declined,
Rise and Shine, its coffee time.

Who Am I

I am me and it's very pleasant,
Rejoicing the past, I live in present.

Liable for my strokes, whatever may come,
dancing to the beats of my own drum.

Confidence is my ability,
My happiness, my responsibility.

As you need air to breathe,
I need some time alone,
Time to be with me,
to write, to feel strong.

Writing gives words to my silence,
Answers to my questions,
Shape to my expression,
Reality to my fantasy.

I won't insult me,
by envying you,
You are splendid,
I compliment you.

There are lots of people,
I respect, I admire,
I am me,
myself lighting my fire.

Anu Girdhar

My improvement begins with I,
As I sing, dance and sway,
A better me is on the way.

Love. We All Need

Neither money nor power can meet,
When love and care is their only need,
Hunger for love, hunger for that silent touch,
Hunger for warm hugs,
Someone who doesn't see your faults,
Soul needs that love and warmth,
People may vary in caste and creed,
Care and share they all need,
Love can cure this loneliness,
despair and greed.

Anu Girdhar

Proud To Be A Prosthodontist

We the Prosthodontists
We are the replicators and the recreators,
Art and science we do combine,
We are the creators of lifeless things
which act life like,
A new smile we perfectly align.

Expert Prosthodontists, that's we are,
No wonder our patients come from far and wide,
They seek our special care to guide,
We give them prosthesis and bring
life to their smiles.
The smiles that set everything right.

Great work comes from great joy,
It's not only our job,
It's our art, our craft,
which we thoroughly enjoy.

Being Prosthodontist, jaw relation is the most vital
relation in our world,
We use this to create smiles with innovative
approach and personalized touch.

My Aging Parents

My aging dad and mom,
As they sit and stare at clock,
Wishing and wanting their children to call,
Waiting for them to come,
Knowing their visits will be short,
But full of laughter and snort.

I got so occupied in my life that I forgot,
My loving parents were growing old.

The love, the compassion and my friendship
they need the most,
One day I will also be, where they are,
As I get older, I start to understand this
more and more.

My children and my parents get along the most,
As both are innocent and soft,
Elder ones, the most experienced,
younger ones, the most pure.

Love your aging parents, be with them,
Shower them with love and care,
One day you will miss them so much,
When you will see their empty chair.

Taking good care of them is our greatest
responsibility,
Loving them, who once showered their love on us
is one of the highest honours.

My Girl

My daughter, a gift of my love,
Raising you was like growing a flower.

You came like a miracle,
Just a look at you, stole my heart.
I found an angel in you, when you learnt to walk,
You made me cry when you left for the
first day of school,
I cried even, when you went for the
first dance class.

My beautiful girl, I don't see passage of time,
I can still see my little girl running
through backyard.

Now you are my best critic, my best friend,
Sometimes I wonder, you grew up fast.
You turned up in a fine young lady,
who is confident, independent and smart,
You know, that's my biggest reward.

You outgrew my lap,
But remember, you will never outgrow my heart.
I never want you to follow my footsteps,
I want you to explore your own path.

In your journey, I shall support you, guide you,
And let you do whatever you want.
It's only me who will tell you about the
life's hardest paths,
I know sometimes to you, I seem unfair and harsh.

I wish you strength, the wisdom,
I want you to never settle for less,
I want you to reach the stars.
I love you and will always do,
Mom and her girl are always close,
In distance they might be apart.

My Son

The moment they placed you in my arms,
You cuddled up right into my heart.

For those precious memories of your childhood,
There is a special place in my heart.
The memories of your laughter,
The sight of your tears,
So beautiful, those few years,
But oh!
How quickly they passed,
My little boy grew up fast.

No longer you are at my side,
For your secrets to confide,
Your toys, your books are put away,
There are no longer games to play,
Now my lap may be too small,
I might not be able to carry you in my arms.
But let my love be the light to guide you,
As you walk your own path.

A few things I forgot to tell you,
I have watched you while you were asleep,
Every time you are upset, my heart sinks,
I smile alone, whenever I think,
Of the time that passed with a blink.

I wish you strength and the wisdom
to choose carefully,
Just remember you are braver than you believe,
Stronger than you seem.

I can't promise to be here for the rest of your life,
But I can promise to love you for the rest of mine.

Being A Man

Men,
How less we talk about them,
But is it easy being a man
Man, the pillar of strength,
To protect woman as father, brother, husband, son
and as best friend.
His attributes can be seen in the goals, dreams and
aspirations he trends.

Is it easy for him to work day and night,
To be a shoulder to everyone,
Is it easy for him, when he is expected to sacrifice.

When he doesn't let you know, he is in pain,
Is it easy for him to hide?

Men do cry, get hurt, get scared,
But being a man, he takes control of his
tears and fears.

A real man loves his wife, places his family as the
most important thing in life,
He is the product of humility, hard work and
sacrifice.

How much do we expect from a man,
He is supposed to smile in trouble,

Gather strength from distress,
To take risks, live passionately on behalf of others,
Forgetting that he has his own battles to fight.

Life is not a competition between man and woman,
It's their collaboration which makes the life bright.

If I Could

If I could freeze the time,
I would go in that old time,
When you and me walked in dazzling moonlight,
Hugging each other tight.

If I could freeze the time,
I would give you the ability to see through my eyes,
What you are to me, to make you realise.

If I could freeze the time,
I shall relive my frozen dreams.

If I could freeze the time,
I would stop this night to touch the morning sky,
To feel you, to be with me whole night.

Anu Girdhar

Hand In Hand

No matter how old we get,
I long for the comfort of holding your hand.

Hand in hand, side by side,
We will walk together on the path of life,

Even if the path ends,
Our journey together is not over yet,
Again and again we shall start afresh.

When I hold your hand, its not about
possessiveness,
It's about how we maintain contact
Through an invisible thread,
Listen to the words we never said,
Though our expression might not be perfect.

Our love story isn't like a fairy tale,
With blink of an eye, things might change,
But my love for you is forever and every day,
I will walk with you through thick and thin,
How far and how long I might stay.

Some Time Alone

Some lonely hours, being alone,
To share your deepest secrets,
To share your feelings,
With the most trusted person,
You, your thoughts and your soul.

There is difference,
Being lonely and being alone,
Being alone can add beauty to life,
Being alone helps you to grow, makes you strong,
Sometimes you find yourself in the middle of no
where,
You might find yourself on the paths that are
unknown,
When you laugh the world laughs with you,
But when you cry, you have to cry alone,
So appreciate, express, love your zone,
Its soulful to spend some time alone.

Anu Girdhar

Love

Love, when its presence is felt with just a hand held,
Love is accepting each other's past,
Supporting each other's present,
Love is when the loved one is free to be himself,
And you keep on building the love until the end.

Love is laughing at each other's jokes,
Helping in the kitchen,
Kissing in the rain,
Telling her she is beautiful,
Love is always flowing like a river,
The river that never ends.

The one you can sleep with,
Make love to,
Travel with,
Dream with,
Love is that best friend.

Love isn't a fairytale or a story book,
As love cannot be always perfect.

Love is when you miss your loved one,
when not around,
Your soul feels the absence.

Love is a short word,
Difficult to define,
But easy to spell.

Love is never a relationship,
Love is relating,
It's an ongoing process,
That continues even when the lovers end.

www.ingramcontent.com/pod-product-compliance
Lightning Source LLC
LaVergne TN
LVHW051453170726
843492LV00002B/664